Exotic Birds

COLORING BOOK

Ruth Soffer

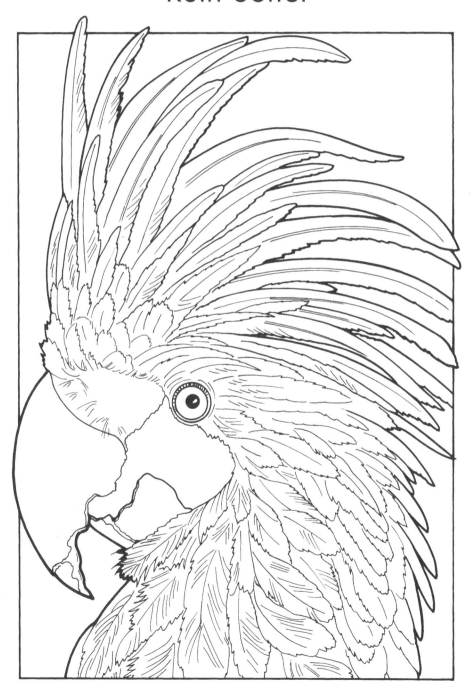

DOVER PUBLICATIONS
GARDEN CITY, NEW YORK

This stunning collection presents in exquisite detail more than thirty exotic birds from around the globe. Depicted in their habitats are the Cassowary, Great Crested Grebe, Magnificent Frigatebird, Scarlet Macaw, and many other species, all awaiting touches of color to make them come alive on the page. Enjoy the distinctive characteristics of each bird as you choose your medium—felt-tip pens, colored pencils, or markers—to produce your own unique images.

Bibliographical Note
Exotic Birds Coloring Book is a new work, first published by Dover Publications in 2015.

International Standard Book Number
ISBN-13: 978-0-486-78337-6
ISBN-10: 0-486-78337-5

Manufactured in the United States of America
78337510   2021
www.doverpublications.com

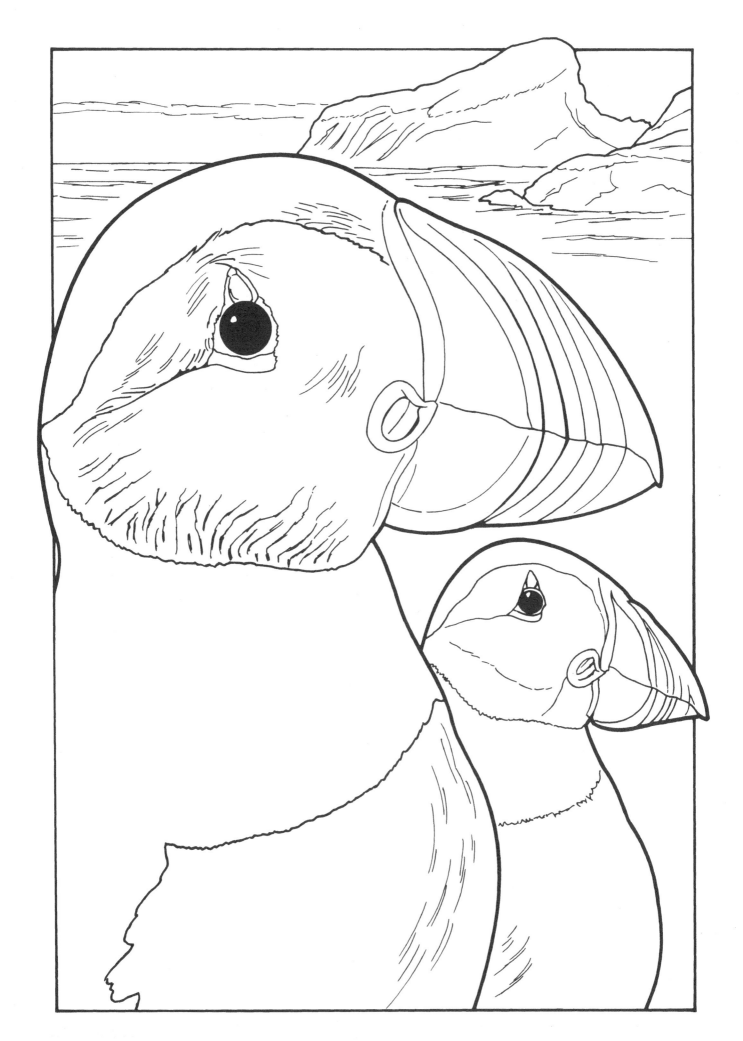

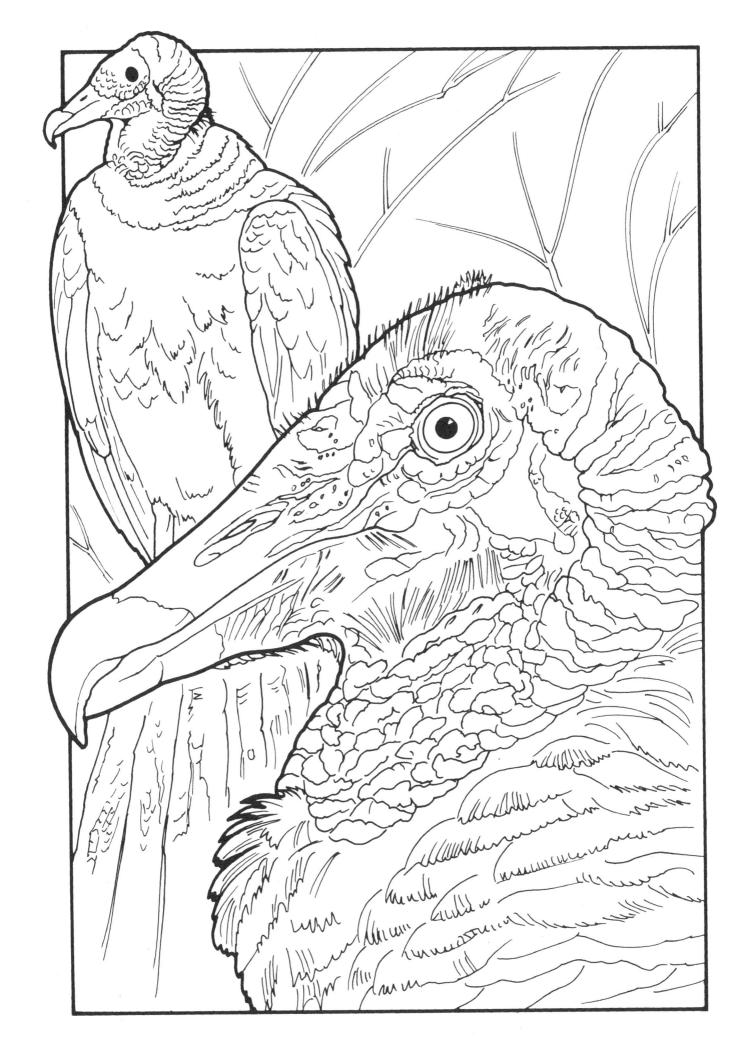

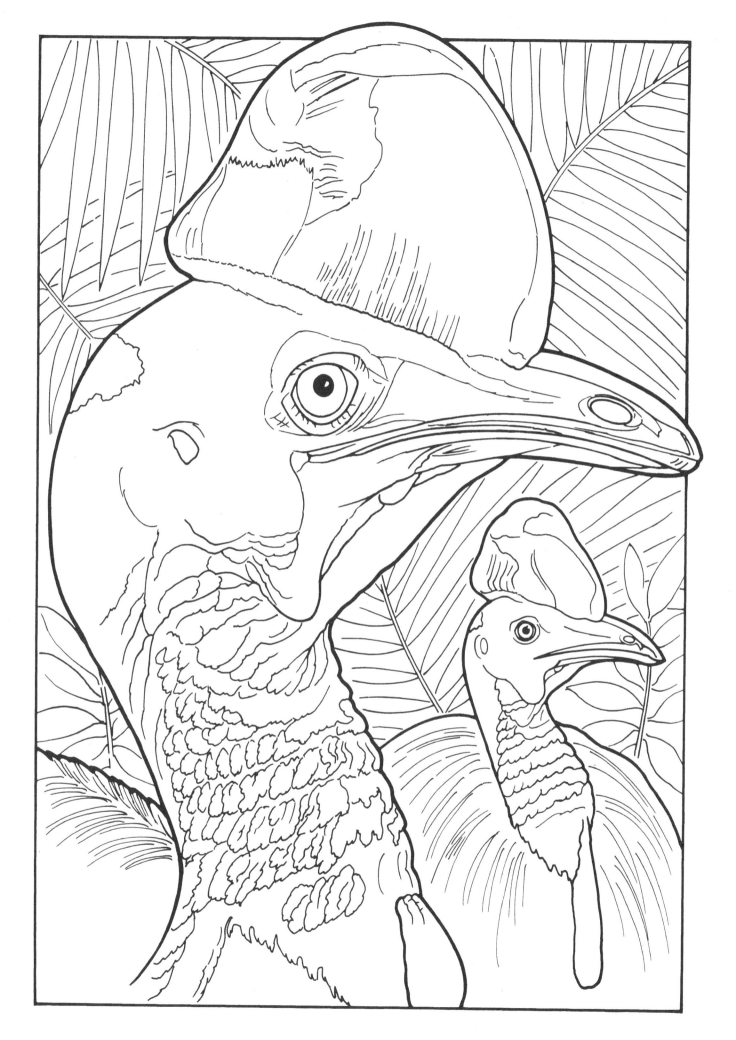

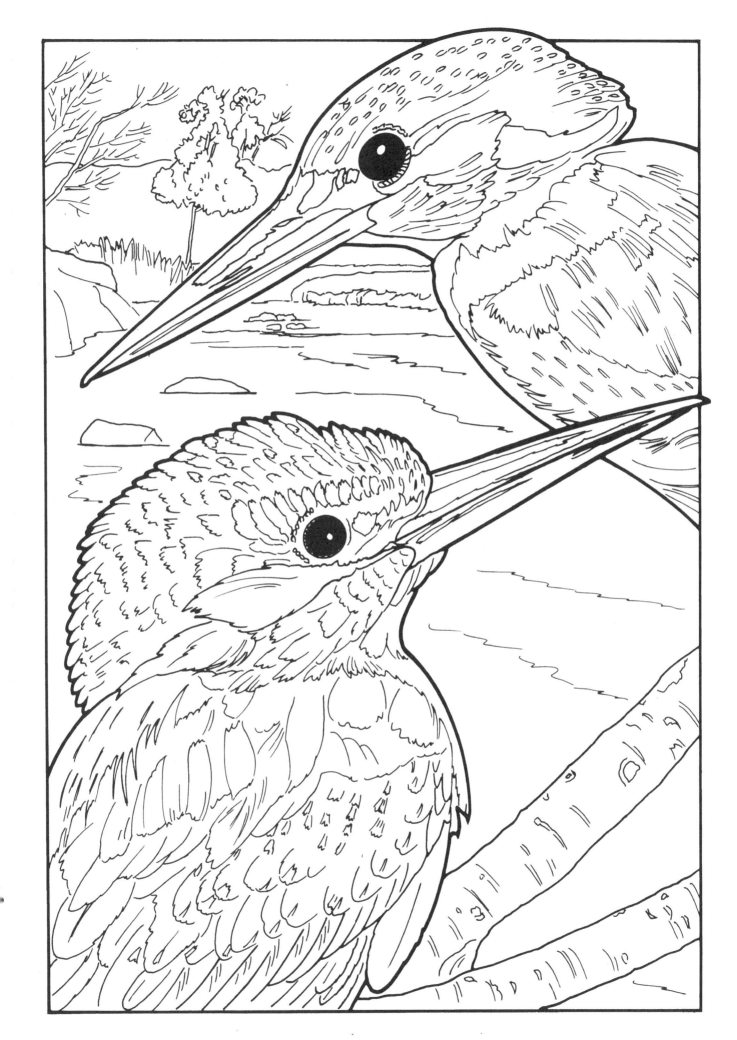

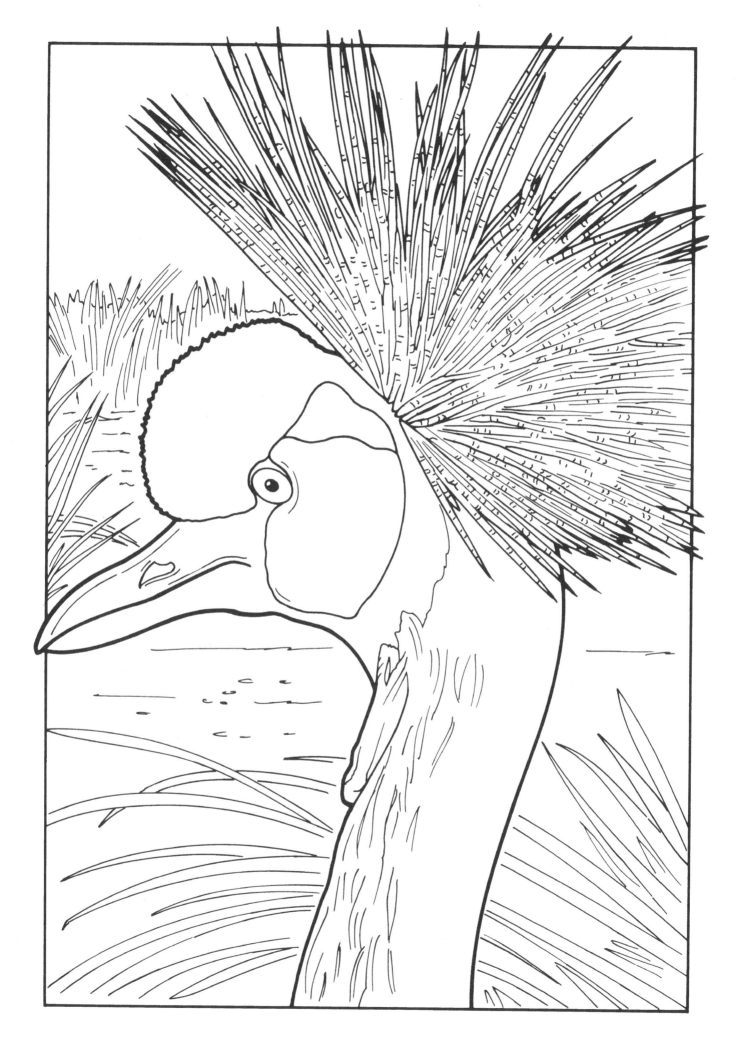

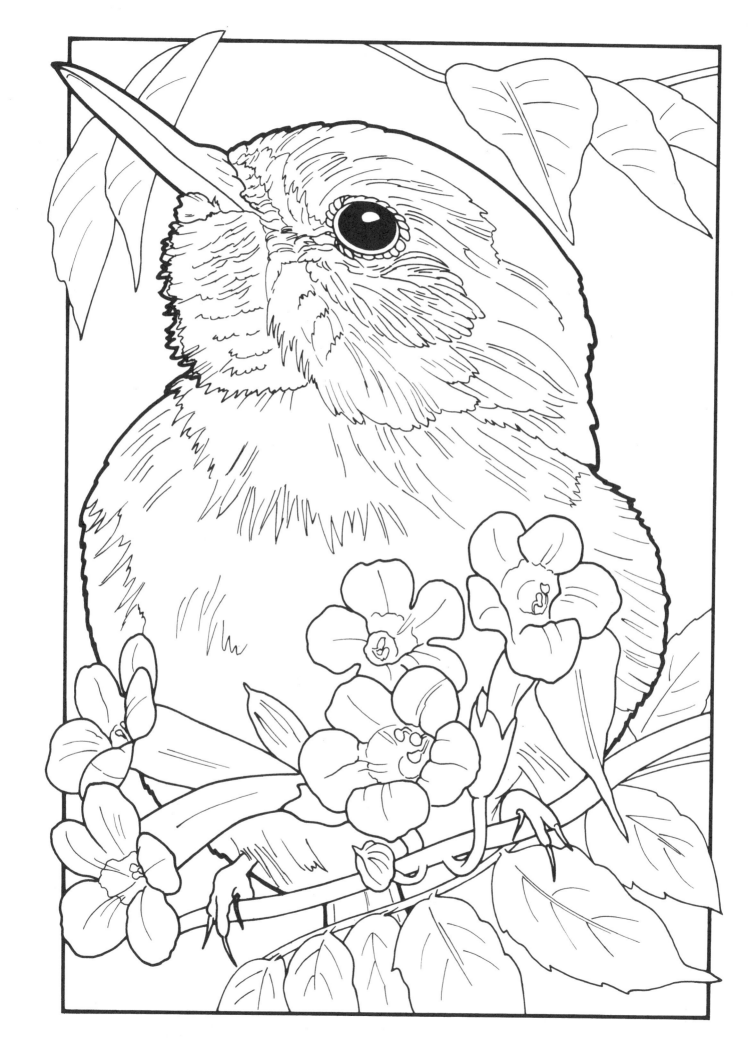

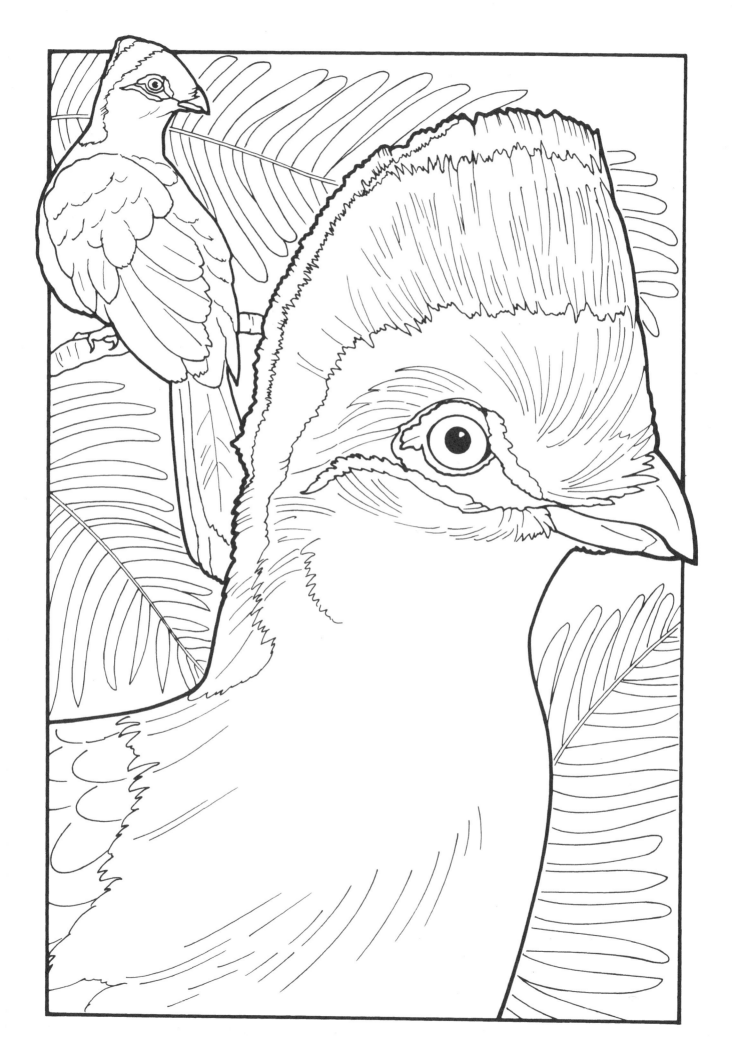

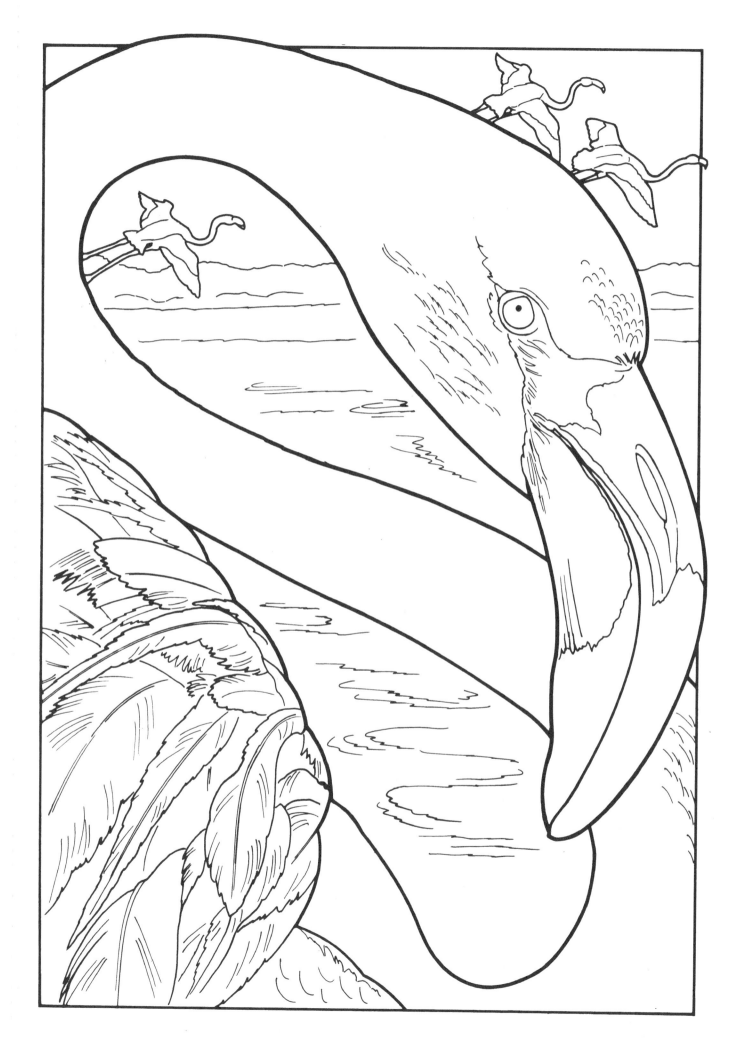

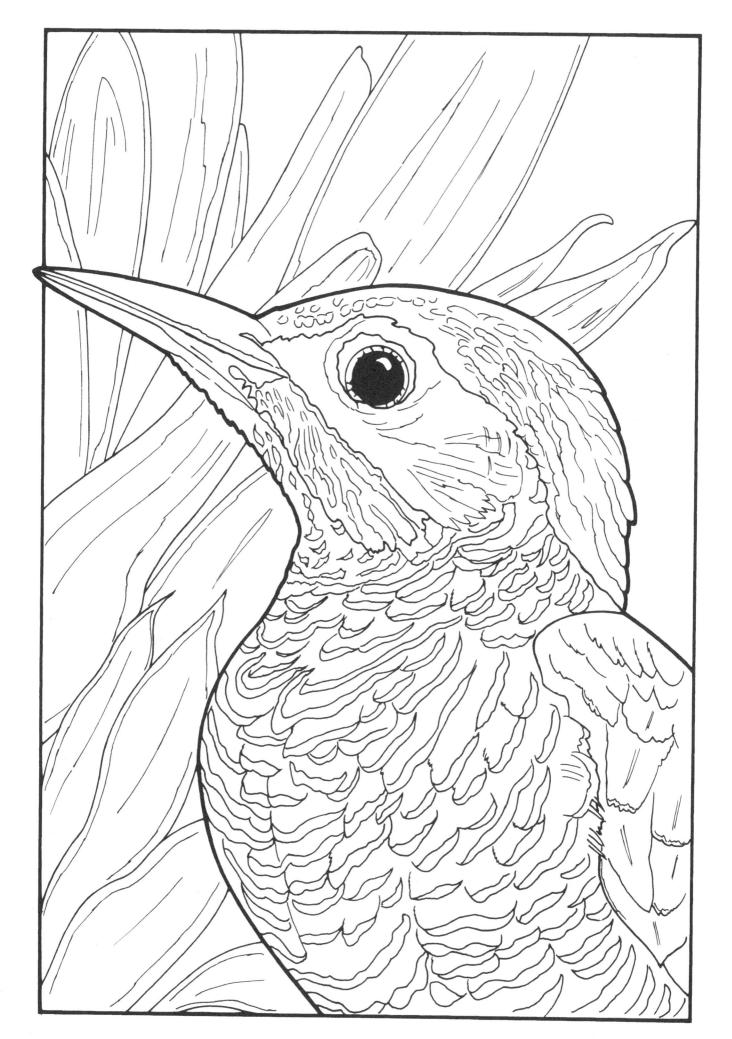

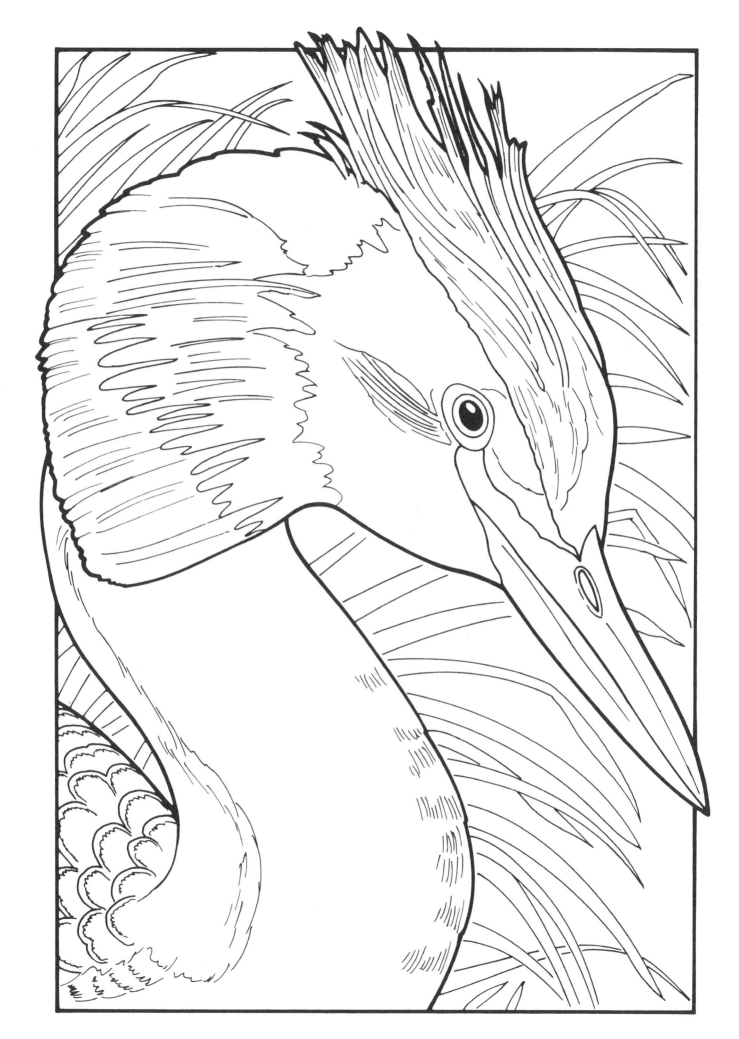

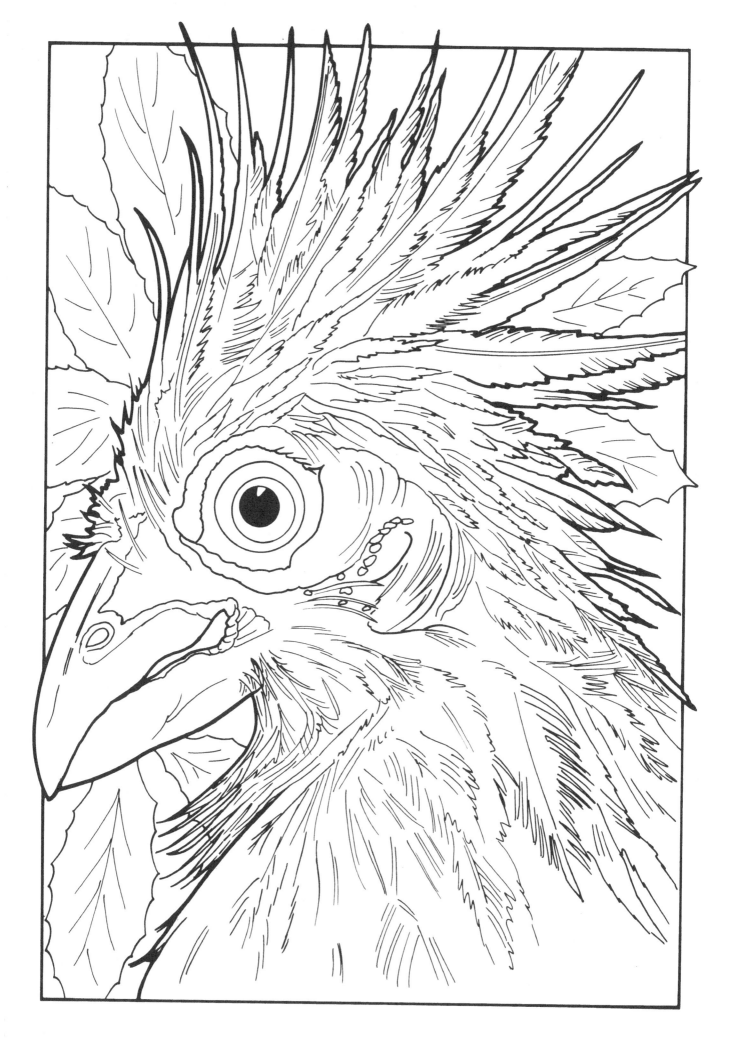

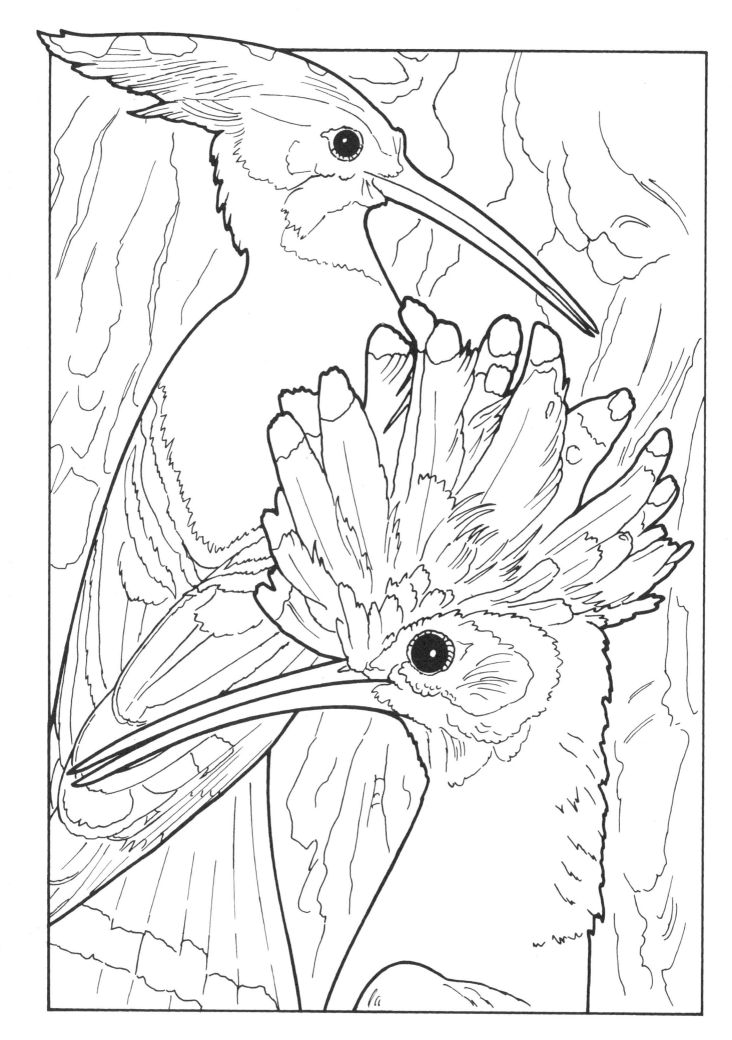

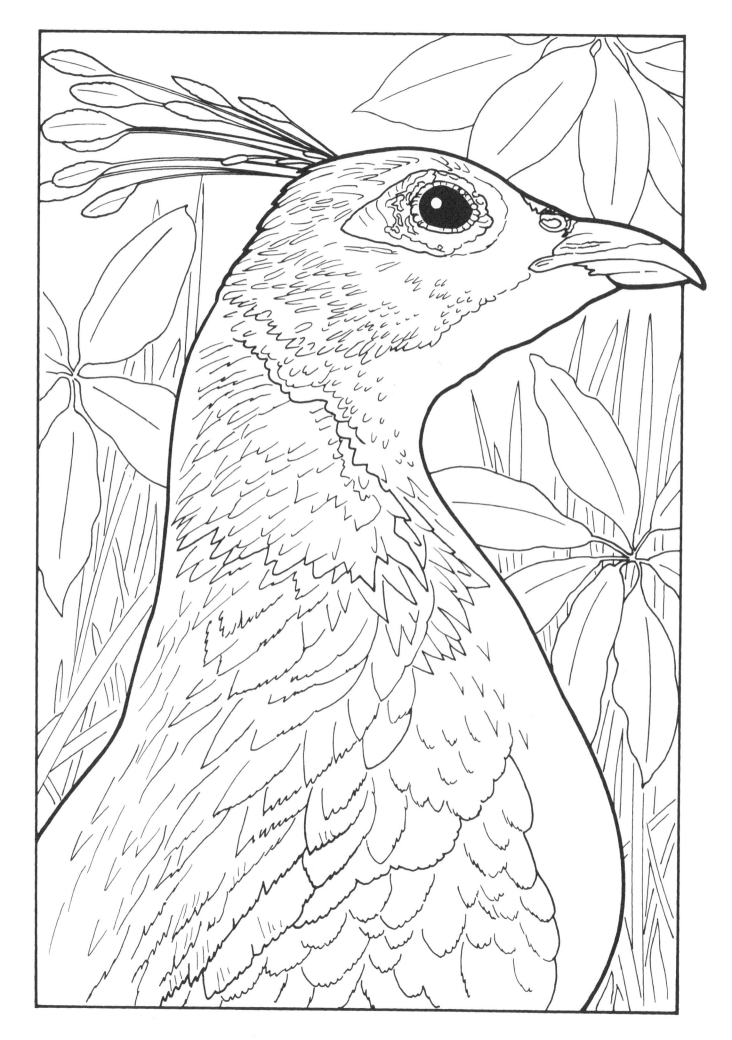

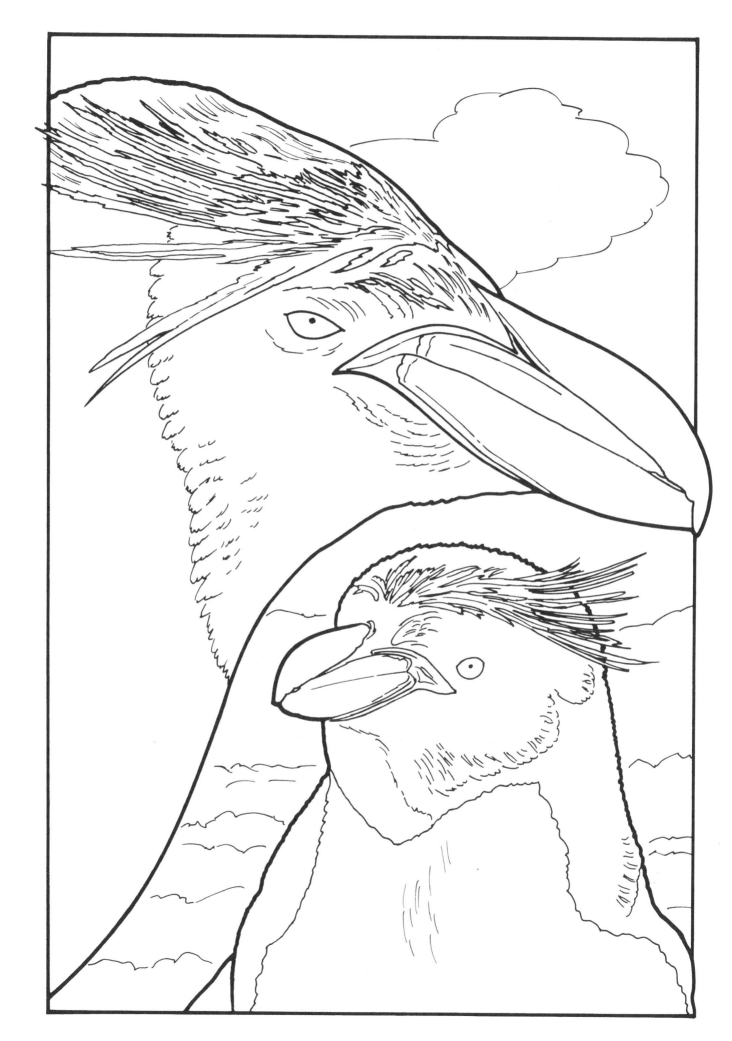

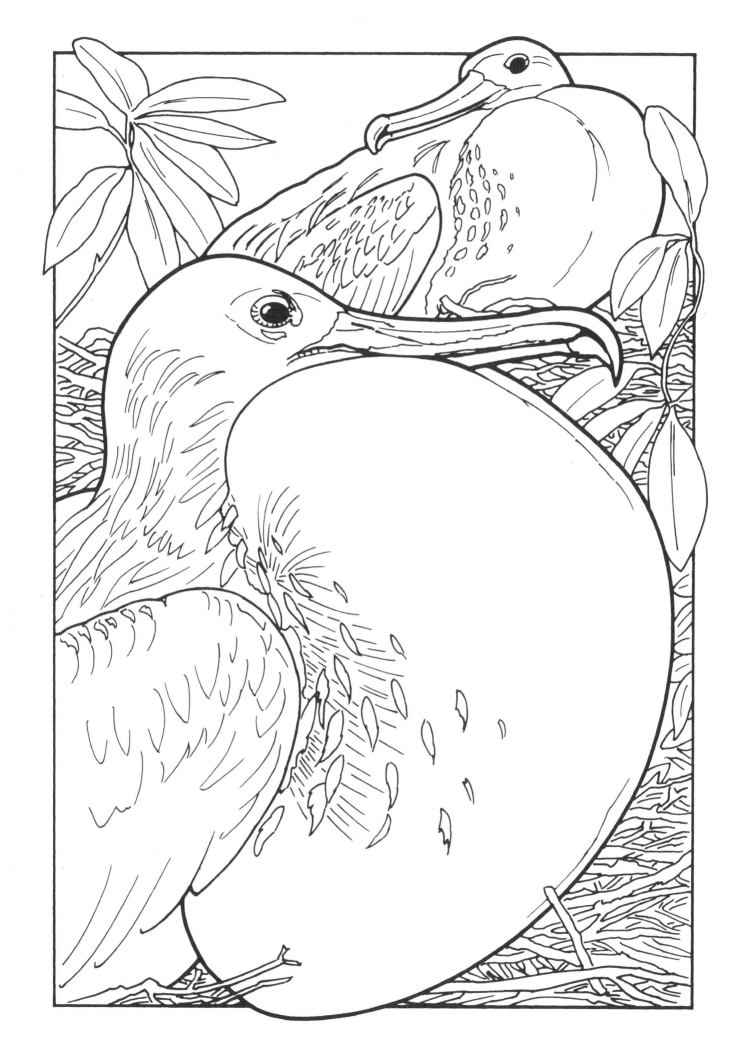

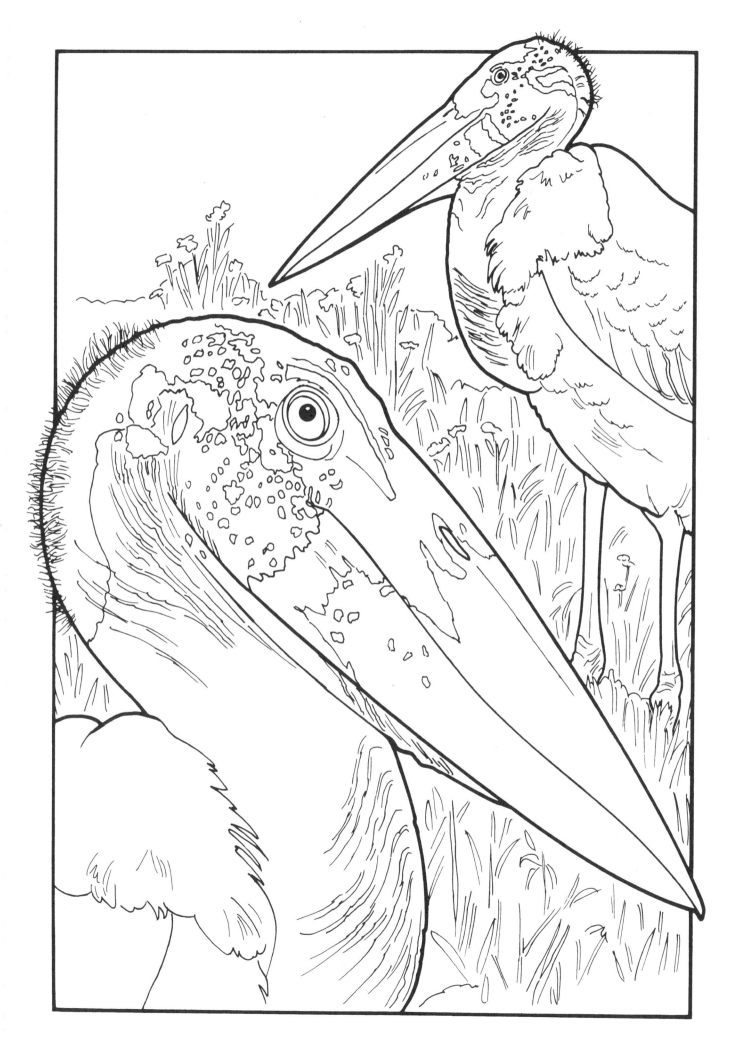

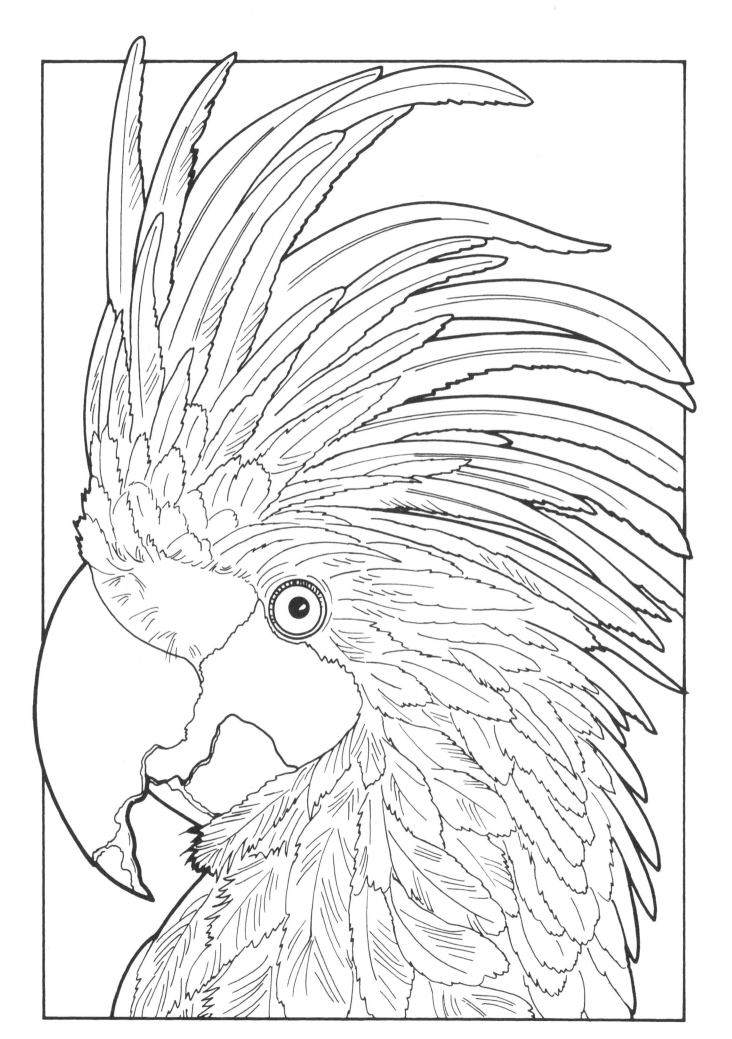

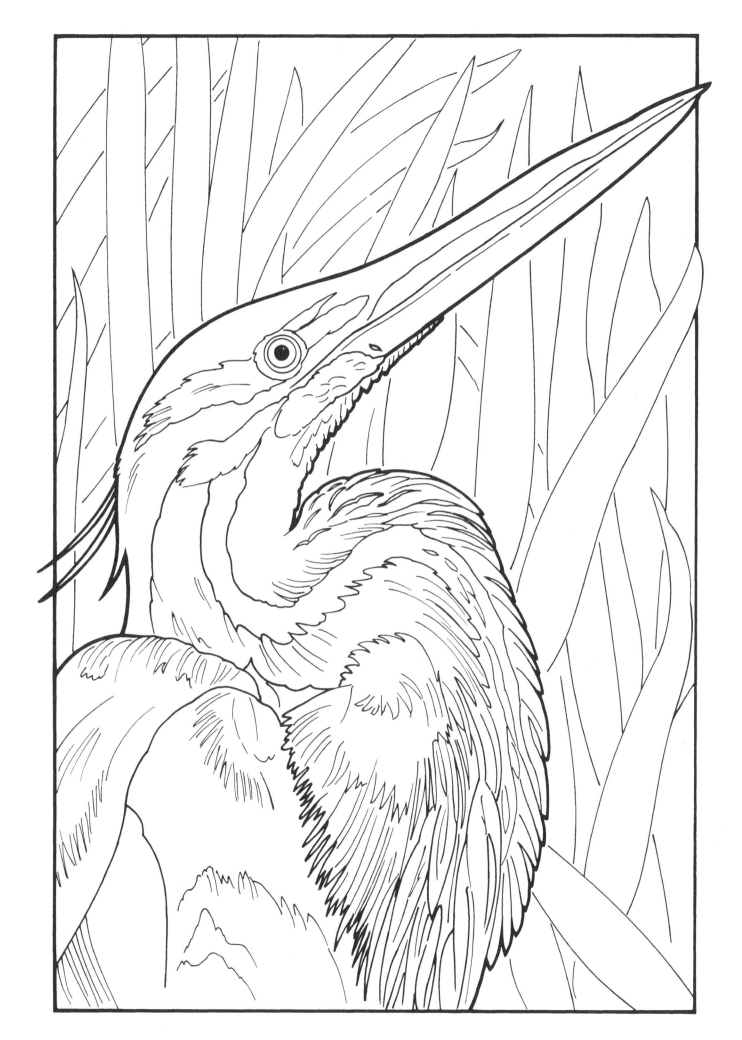

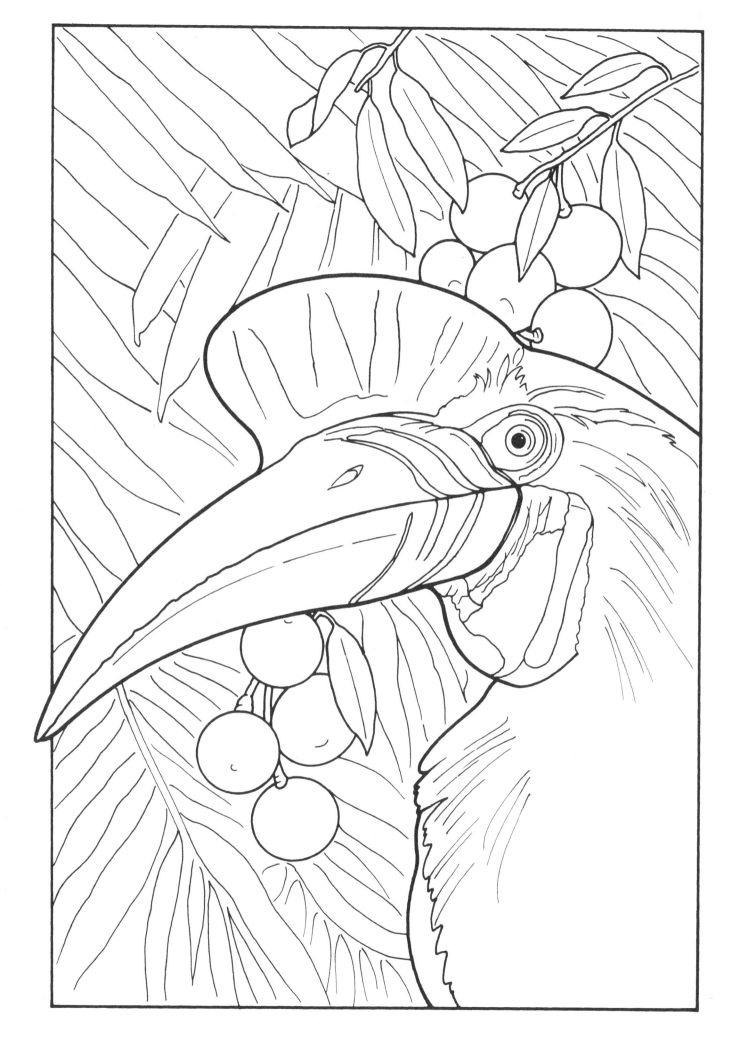

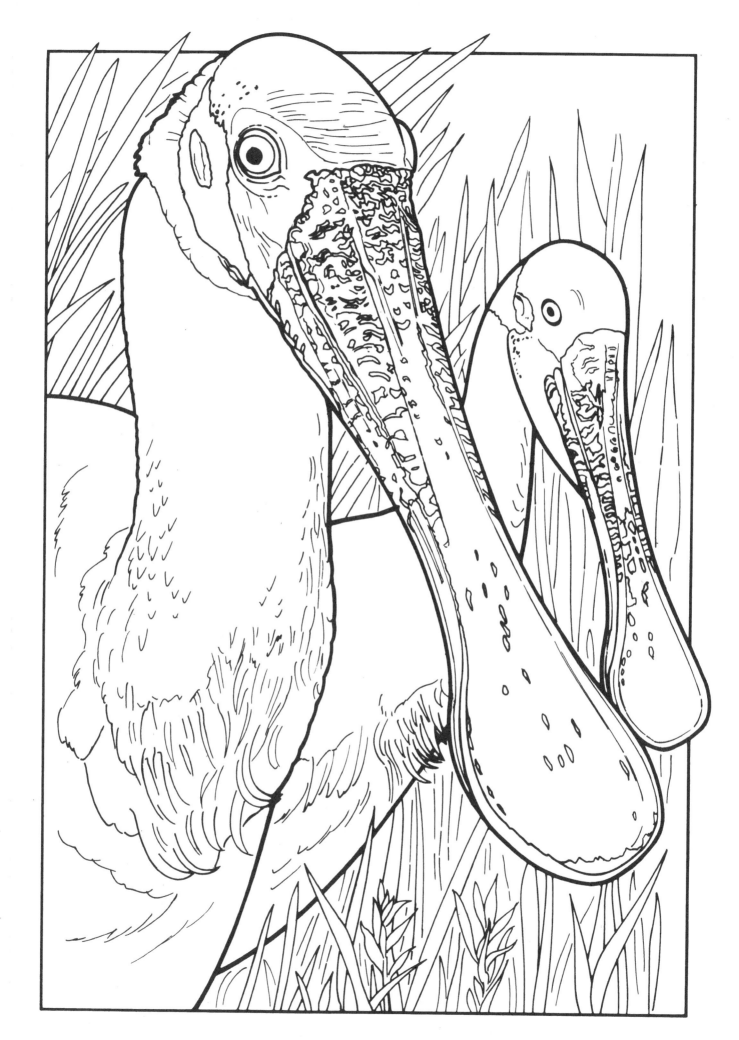

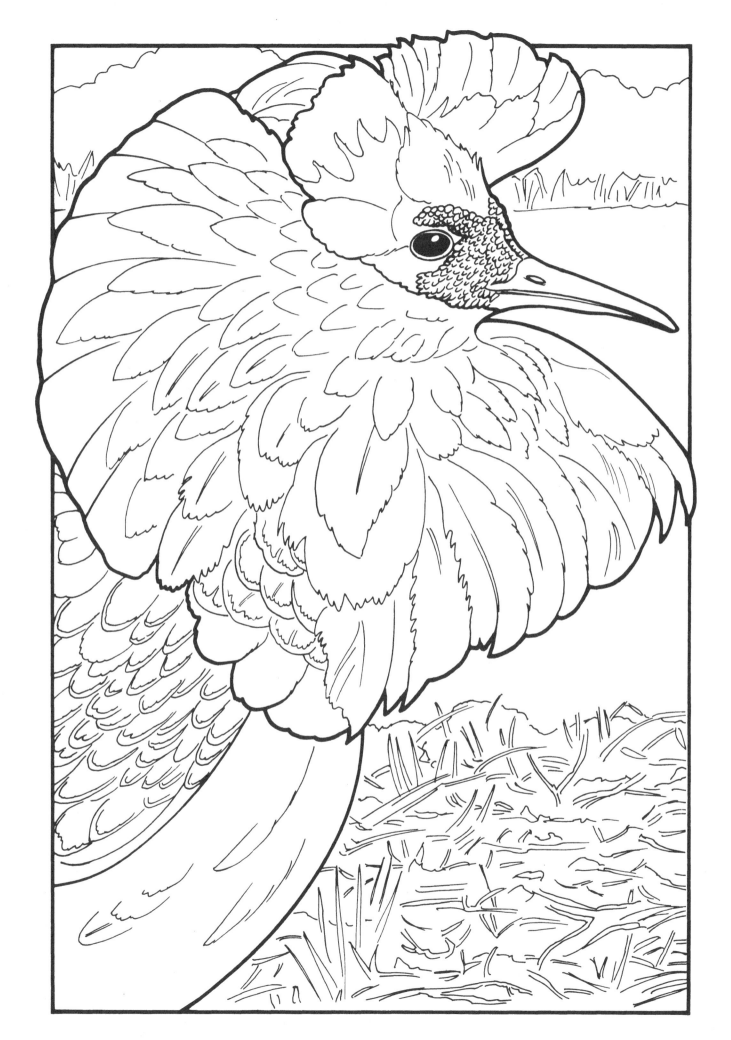

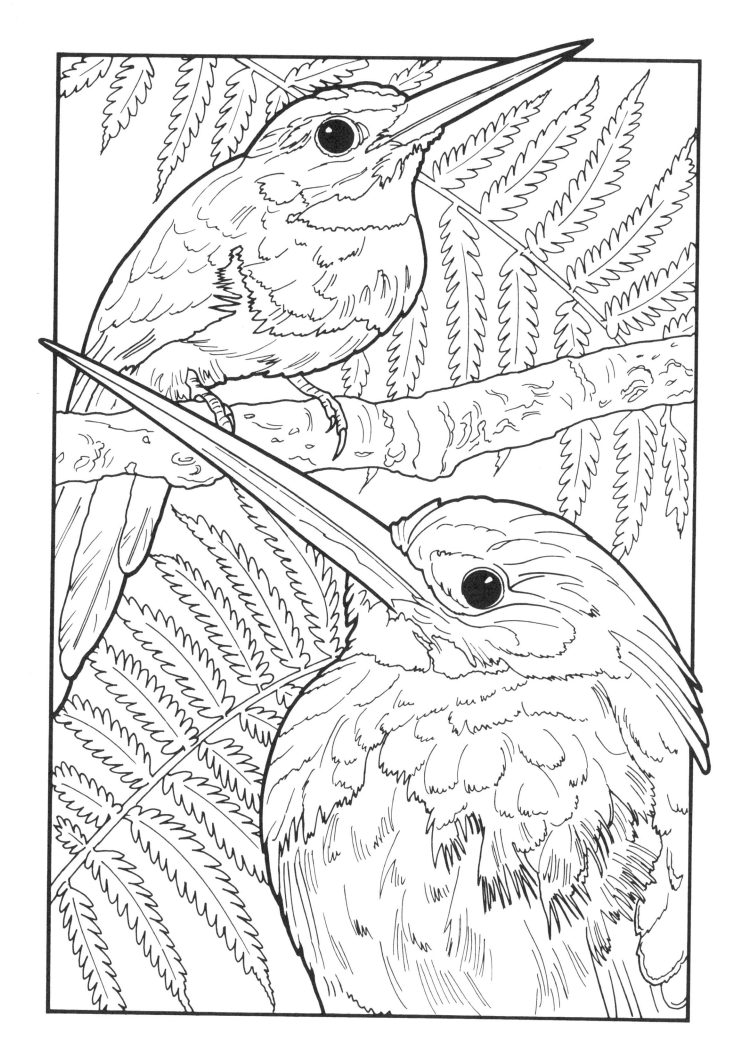

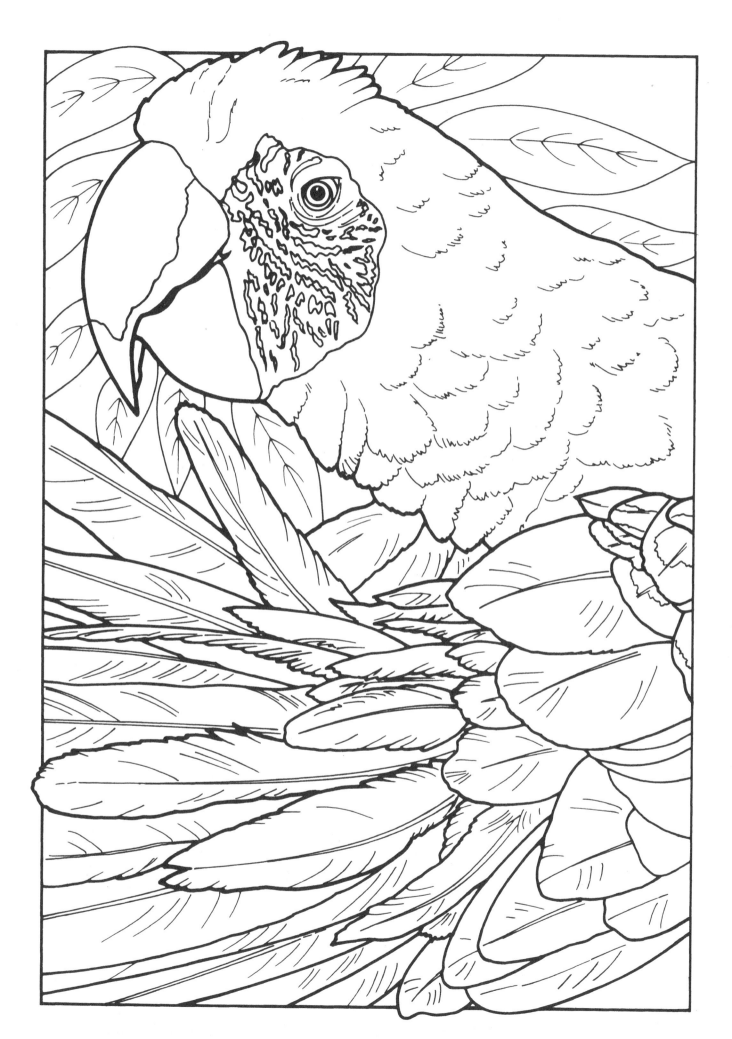

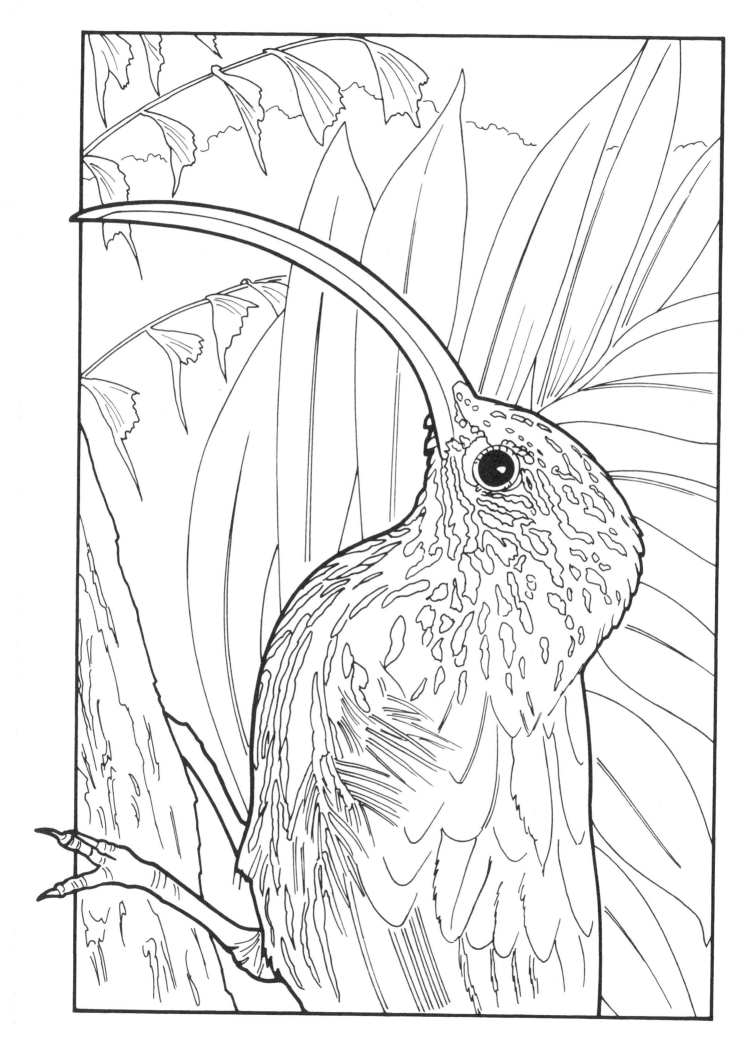

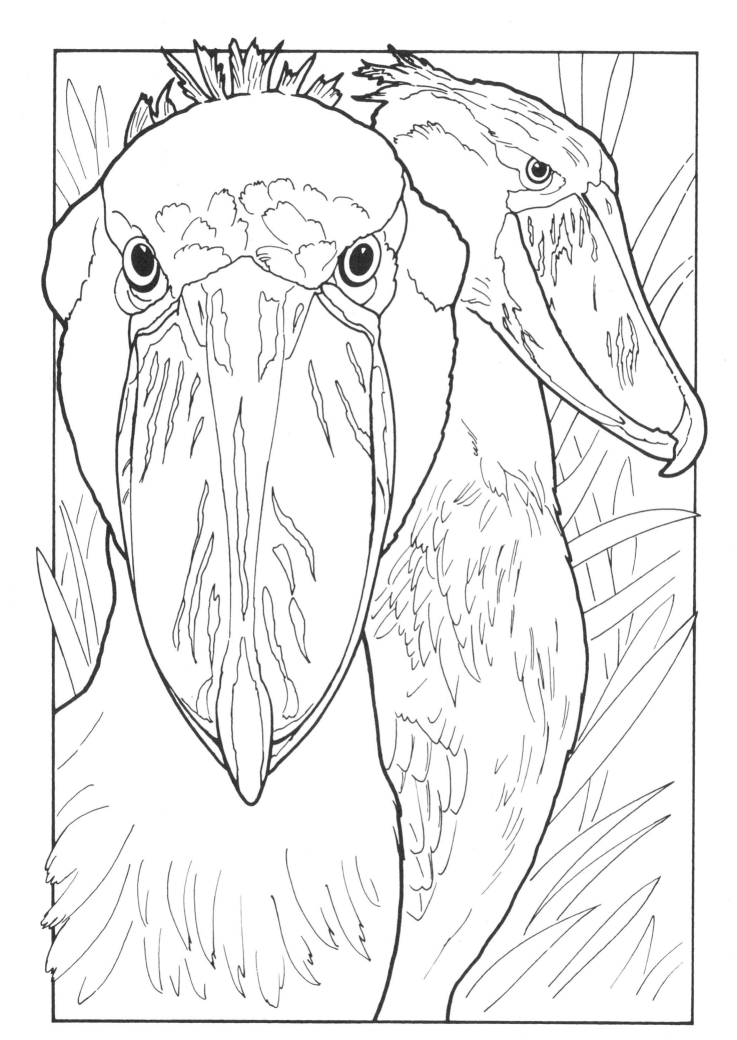

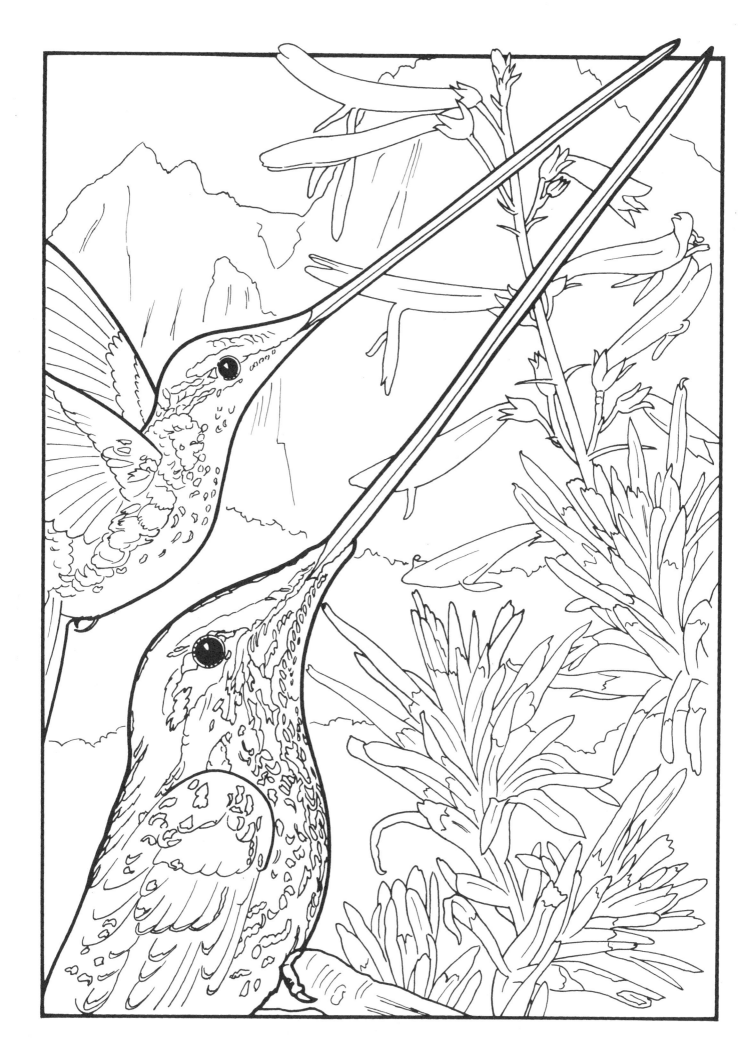

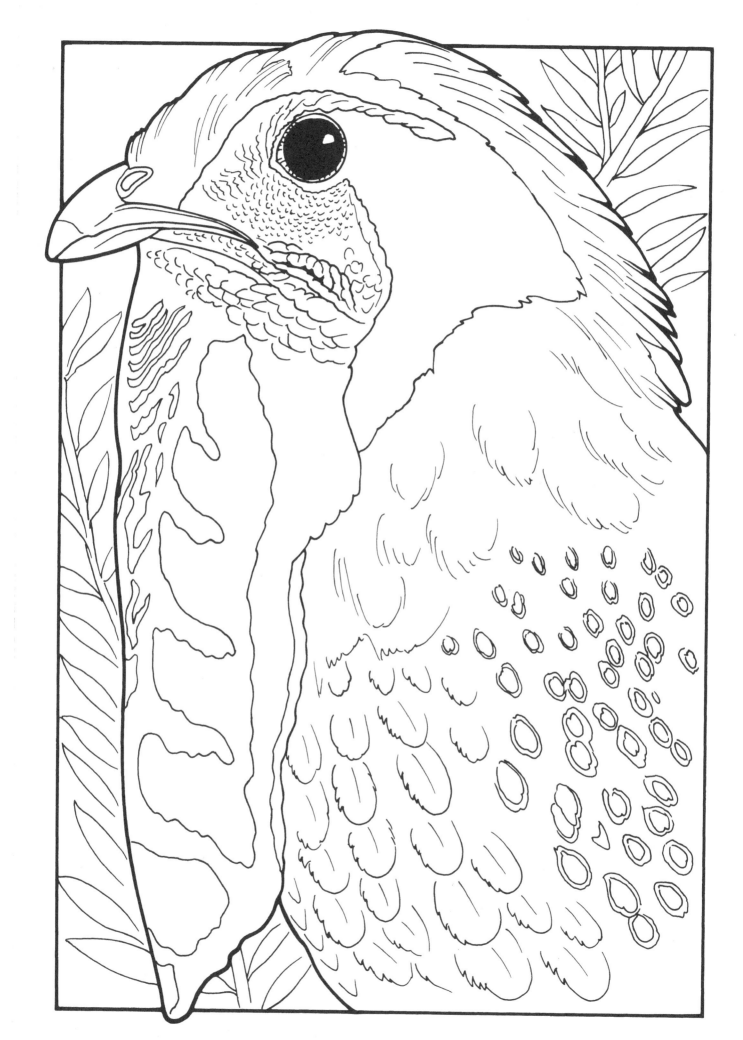

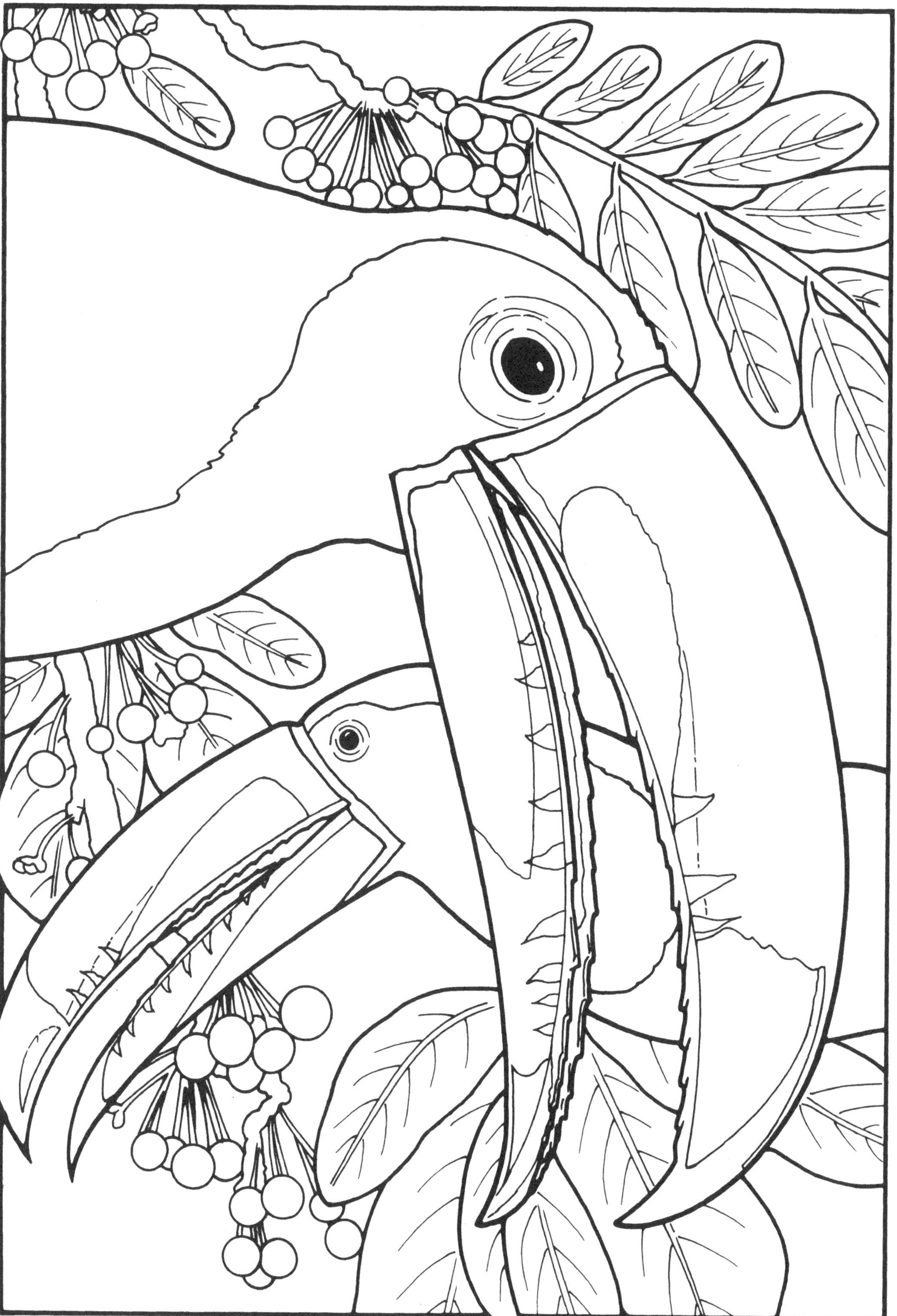

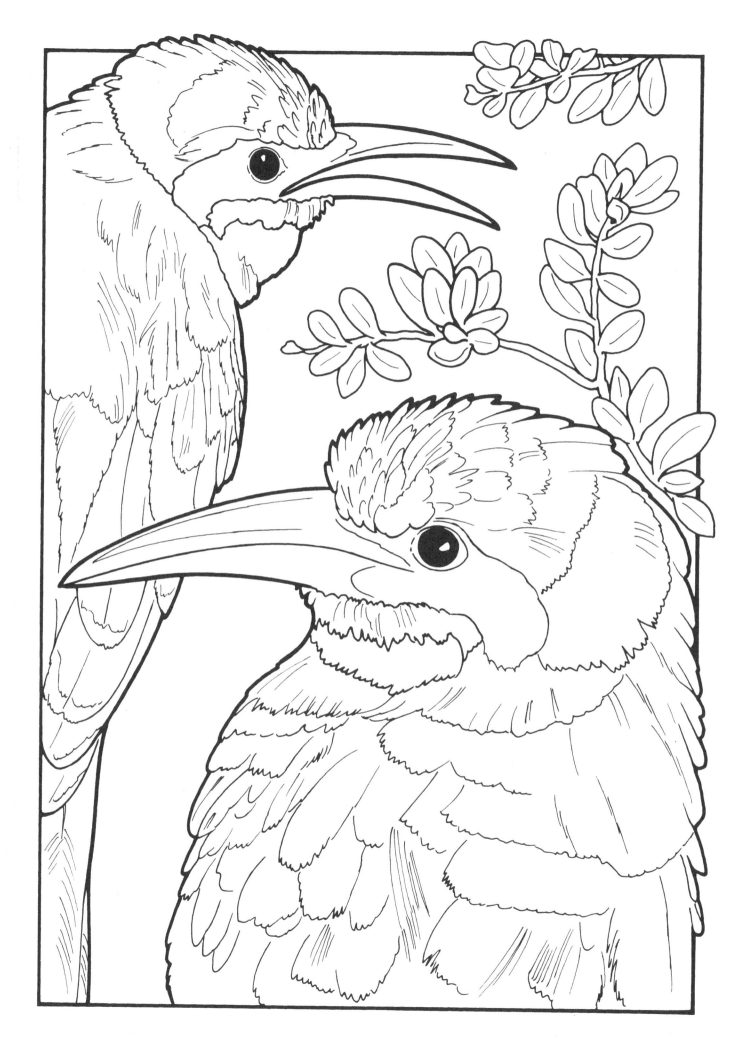

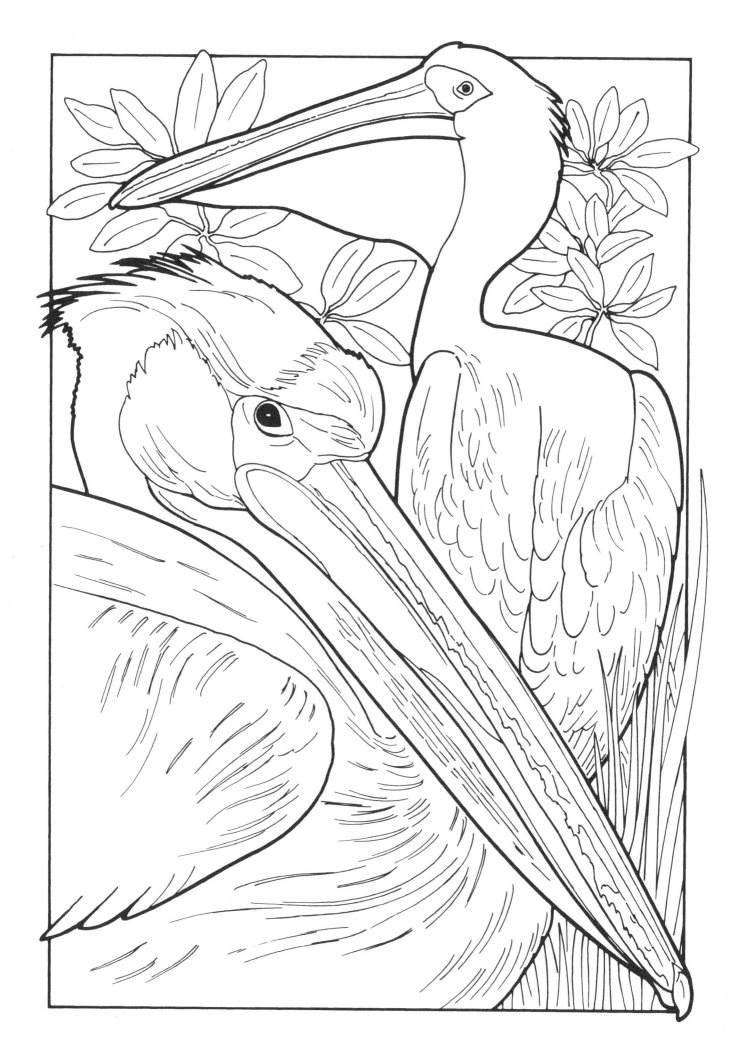

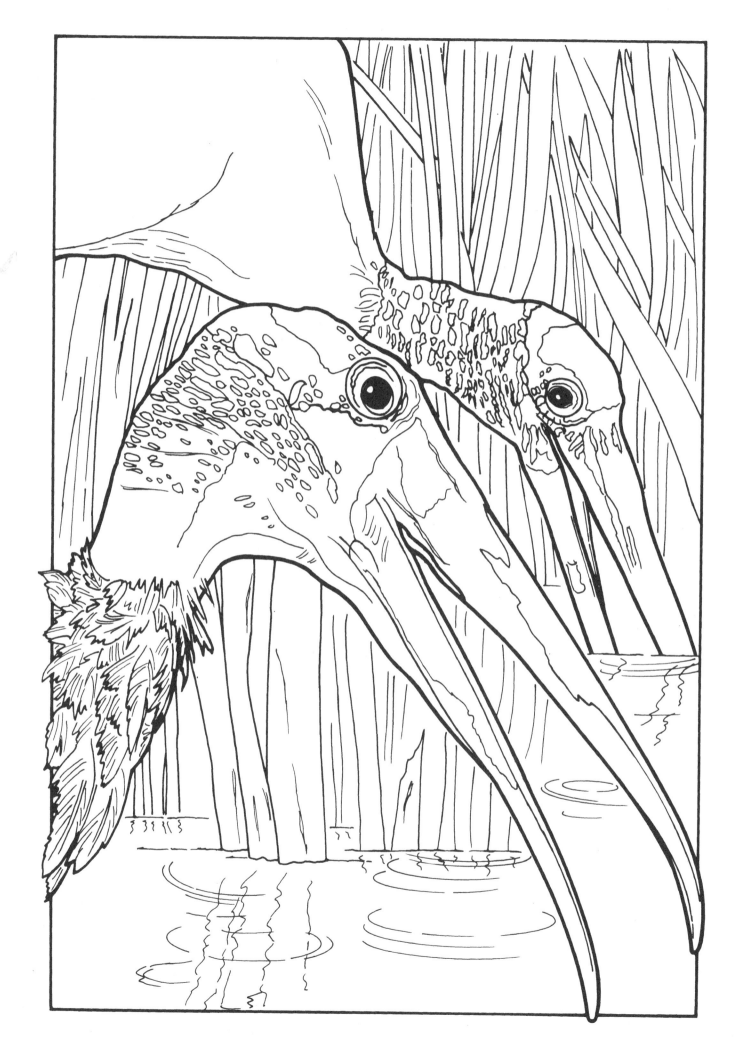